HUNTING: PURSUING WILD GAME! ™

WATERFOWL

PHILIP WOLNY

rosen publishing's
**rosen
central®**

New York

For Dennis Serrano, and the best summer ever

Published in 2011 by The Rosen Publishing Group, Inc.
29 East 21st Street, New York, NY 10010

First Edition

Library of Congress Cataloging-in-Publication Data

Wolny, Philip.
Waterfowl / Philip Wolny. — 1st ed.
    p. cm. — (Hunting: pursuing wild game!)
Includes bibliographical references and index.
ISBN 978-1-4488-1243-1 (library binding) —
ISBN 978-1-4488-2273-7 (pbk.) —
ISBN 978-1-4488-2278-2 (6-pack)
1. Waterfowl shooting—Juvenile literature. I. Title.
SK331.W65 2011
799.2'44—dc22

2010017396

Manufactured in Malaysia

CPSIA Compliance Information: Batch #W11YA: For further information, contact Rosen Publishing, New York, New York, at 1-800-237-9932.

On the cover: Waterfowl hunting, which includes the hunting of migratory birds like this mallard, is a sport, pastime, and proud tradition in many parts of the world.

CONTENTS

For many of us, hunting waterfowl is one of the most fulfilling pastimes. Throughout North America's wetlands, it is not only a sport but also a centuries-old tradition. Older, experienced hunters pass on their knowledge and love of hunting duck and geese to their children. Ask any waterfowl enthusiast, and he or she will be excited to talk about cherished hunting experiences.

While it is a deeply satisfying outdoor activity, under-taken for both food and sport, waterfowl hunting is also serious business. As with any sport, pursuit, or activity, it takes time to build up the confidence and skills necessary to be successful. Even veteran hunters who have pursued waterfowl for many seasons can learn new techniques and lessons with every new outing.

Being a good hunter is not merely a question of skills. Hunters must handle shotguns confidently, responsibly, and safely in order to prevent hurting—or even killing—themselves and/or others in their party. The right equipment and gear will keep a hunter warm and dry and will help ensure a more successful hunt. Proper licenses, stamps, and other certifications will keep hunters in compliance with the law and out of trouble with state and federal authorities. So, too, will

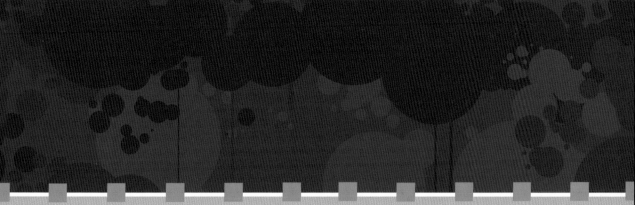

Hunter John Cameron uses a duck call as the sun rises over a wetland area near Auckland, New Zealand.

paying attention to changes in waterfowl hunting regulations. Good planning, maps, and a compass will prevent accidents and injuries and get everyone in the hunting party home safely.

Respect for nature, one's fellow hunters, and the rights of property owners are all important rules to learn and live by. One of the most important of these rules is following state and federal regulations concerning limits on the numbers and types of waterfowl that can be bagged. By living according to an ethical and law-abiding code, hunters have been major players in helping manage wildlife and conserve valuable public lands. A true waterfowl hunter is both a sportsman or sportswoman and an environmentalist, someone who thrills to the hunt but is also a cautious team player.

The aim of this book is to encourage young people to learn how to hunt safely and successfully. With the right equipment, skills, and attitude, they will hopefully hunt safely, ethically, and legally for decades to come and teach their own children and grandchildren how to do so. With that in mind, welcome to the wonderful world of waterfowl hunting!

CHAPTER 1

GETTING STARTED

Long before hunters find themselves wading through the reeds, or in a field ready to take a shot, there are important things to learn and consider. Like other outdoor sporting activities, hunting waterfowl is fun and rewarding. But it is a very serious business, too, that requires careful safety and skills training.

One of the first things any waterfowl hunter needs to do is learn how to shoot. Specifically, beginning hunters must learn how to safely and properly handle a shotgun. This includes learning how to care for and maintain it and use and store it legally. State and federal regulations differ over what gauges of weapon can be used in certain wildlife areas. But there are universal rules about how to behave in the wilderness when armed with a potentially lethal weapon. Most of these rules follow the dictates of simple common sense.

Iowa Department of Natural Resources recreational safety officer Jeff Barnes teaches students who are taking a mandatory ten-hour hunter education course in Ames, Iowa.

Some readers may already be familiar with guns and hunting. Still, even if they have hunted deer, turkey, or other game, they may be new to hunting waterfowl. Even seasoned pros need to review the basics occasionally in order to stay sharp and focused and avoid developing bad habits. As a result, this chapter will hopefully prove useful to both beginners and those who have already gotten their feet wet, so to speak.

Hunter Education and Safety Courses

All fifty U.S. states require that new hunters complete some kind of hunter safety course. In most places, such courses are provided free of charge and are funded by the state's fish and wildlife service.

Let's imagine that a young person in North Carolina wants to go hunting. The wildlife resources commission schedules a hunter education course several times a year in each county of the state. There is no minimum age for the course, which is taught by wildlife enforcement officers and skilled volunteers. In this class, students will learn about wildlife conservation, hunter responsibility and safety, firearms, identifying wildlife, first aid and survival, and other important aspects of hunting. All first-time hunting license buyers must take the course.

Another example is provided by South Dakota, where a similar introductory hunting course is called HuntSAFE. It is offered for those between twelve and fifteen years of age, who earn a hunter safety certification card. Under federal guidelines, students take at least ten hours of instruction in handling firearms. They also learn hunting safety, ethics, and the proper relationship among hunters, wildlife, and conservation. They complete a written test and often do live-fire exercises under instructor supervision.

Once the course is passed, anyone under sixteen must be accompanied by an adult to obtain a Youth Small Game License and a Migratory Bird Certification. The fees for the license and certification are only a few dollars each. It is important to remember that rules and fees vary among all the states. The following chapter will cover licenses and other certifications in greater detail.

Mentors and Teachers

Young people new to waterfowl hunting usually have a parent, older sibling, or other relative, such as an uncle, or friends of the family with whom they go out on hunts. There are many different rules all over North America dictating the minimum ages for hunting alone and hunting with an adult.

For obvious reasons, it is a bad idea for someone with very little experience to go shooting alone, regardless of age. Yet even young

Because waterfowl hunting is a tradition passed down from generation to generation, children gain invaluable knowledge and experience by learning from mentors like parents, older siblings, and other hunting veterans.

people who are expert marksmen still need the guidance and supervision of experienced adults. That's why rules in every state require that if a hunter is under a certain age, he or she must be accompanied by someone eighteen years or older.

Getting practice, instruction, advice, and guidance from an experienced adult before hitting the field is a great way to get comfortable with a shotgun. Going to a local shooting range, or some other place where it is legal and safe to target-shoot, is also a great idea.

Youth Waterfowl Days

Many states and waterfowl hunting organizations actively promote youth hunting so that the next generation preserves and passes on the traditions and rules of the sport. To do so, they are promoting youth waterfowl hunts on designated weekends during the hunting season. Such hunts may include a day of instruction on hunting and gun safety, the proper use of shotguns, bird identification, ecology, hunting tactics, and other outdoor training.

Choosing Your Weapon

One of the first things a young hunter learns is that only shotguns are used in waterfowling. Rifles of any kind are illegal for this particular kind of hunting. Generally, a shotgun is fired from the user's shoulder. Unlike a rifle, which fires bullets, shotguns shoot small round projectiles, or pellets, called shot, or a single solid projectile called a slug.

Shotguns are usually smoothbore weapons. This means the interior of the gun barrel is smooth, unlike rifles. The word "rifle" actually refers to the grooves—the rifles—in the barrel that help direct bullets with greater accuracy when fired.

A hunter wearing a safety vest holds a pump-action shotgun. The choice of a hunting weapon is an important one and depends on many factors, including age, experience, and personal preferences.

At close range, shotguns are very powerful. Because shot spreads when fired, shotguns are effective against small and moving targets—like waterfowl—because they don't require the hunter to aim with pinpoint accuracy. Shot becomes less effective and powerful at longer ranges. Shotguns are either single-barreled semiautomatic or pump-action weapons or double-barreled side-by-side or over/under guns. A semiautomatic shotgun can eject spent cartridges and fire a new one after every trigger squeeze without requiring manual reloading. A pump-action shotgun uses a pump to eject spent cartridges and reload after each shot. In side-by-side shotguns, the two-barrels are next to each other. With over/under guns, one barrel is stacked upon the other. With double-barreled shotguns, spent cartridges must be removed and new ones loaded manually after two shots.

Gauging Your Needs

When we talk about different types of shotguns, we generally refer to their gauge. "Gauge" refers to the diameter of the shotgun's bore and the shot used as ammunition. The smaller the gauge number, the larger the bore. The three gauge sizes most common in waterfowl hunting, from largest to smallest bore, are 10 gauge, 12 gauge, and 20 gauge. Each type of shotgun only uses shot appropriate to its gauge; a 12 gauge only takes 12-gauge shot, for example.

The Ten Commandments of Firearms Safety

The Ten Commandments of Firearms Safety are an invaluable reminder of some basic, commonsense gun dos and don'ts. Learn them and live them.
1. Always keep the muzzle pointed in a safe direction.
2. Firearms should be unloaded when not actually in use.
3. Don't rely on your gun's safety catch.
4. Be sure of your target and what's beyond it.
5. Use proper ammunition.
6. If your gun fails to fire when the trigger is pulled, handle with care.
7. Always wear eye and ear protection when shooting.
8. Be sure the barrel is clear of obstructions before shooting.
9. Don't alter or modify your gun, and be sure to have it serviced regularly.
10. Learn the mechanical and handling characteristics of the firearm you are using.

Source: Remington Arms Company, Inc.

While the 10 gauge is the largest shotgun used for waterfowl and can kill ducks up to a sixty-yard (fifty-five-meter) distance, it is also heavier and has greater recoil. Recoil is the amount of force pushing back on the hunter after he or she takes a shot. As a result, the most common choice for waterfowling is a 12-gauge shotgun.

Twenty-gauge guns are often the best pick for younger or inexperienced hunters. Beginners should avoid guns with stronger recoil until they have developed their shooting skills and strength. Younger and less experienced gun users are often unprepared for the strength of the recoil. The force of it can lead to injury and even shooting accidents.

Shells used for duck hunting contain shot. The mix of materials affects the way shot behaves when fired from a shotgun.

Unleaded Only

In the past, lead shot was commonly used by waterfowl hunters. However, it was eventually discovered that ducks and geese (among many other birds and other animal species) were ingesting leftover lead shot, mainly from lake and river bottoms. Lead poisoning is harmful not only to the animals, but also to those who dine on duck and geese.

As a result, all birdshot used in North American wetland areas must now be nontoxic. Nonlead alternatives include steel, bismuth-tin, and mixed-metal shot using tungsten, nickel, and iron, among others. The cheapest alternative is steel. Yet many hunters note that because steel is less dense than lead and other metals, it has a lower velocity and therefore a reduced effective range. Tungsten, bismuth, and other materials are as dense or denser than lead, but are more expensive than steel. Still, shotgun manufacturers have worked on making higher muzzle velocities for their guns, with some success.

CHAPTER 2

BEFORE THE HUNT: LAWS AND REGULATIONS, ETHICS AND RESPONSIBILITIES

*H*unting waterfowl is a cherished pastime and a revered tradition that is founded upon and sustained by a hunter's code of ethics and state and federal laws. These laws are all designed to ensure the safety of hunters and the health of waterfowl populations and their habitats. For if the waterfowl disappear due to poor hunting and ecological practices, so, too, will waterfowl hunting disappear. Young waterfowlers must make sure they learn and respect the various rules and regulations governing the hunting of duck and geese.

Licenses, Permits, and Stamps

For new hunters, it may seem that there is a great deal of official paperwork involved before they can get out and bag their first mallard. The good news is that many of these forms and applications can be filled out and submitted online. In addition, hunting licenses, stamps, and permits can be obtained in person at a variety of locations: fish and wildlife offices, gun shops, the post office, and other certified locations.

Pure Michigan Hunt (www.michigan.gov/dnr) is a special program of the state's Department of Natural Resources and Environment designed to promote hunting. Many states hold special hunts to encourage young hunters to take up the sport.

A hunter's best bet is to check with his or her state's fish and wildlife service, whether online or in person, to learn what paperwork must be completed and where it can be filled out and submitted.

After successfully completing a hunter safety course, most young people must be accompanied in the field by a properly licensed adult hunter (over the age of eighteen). This means a parent, guardian, or other responsible adult. Rules vary by state, so hunters must be sure to familiarize themselves with the regulations and requirements of the area in which they will be hunting (whether in their home state or elsewhere).

In Wyoming, for example, only those sixteen or older need a duck stamp to hunt waterfowl, but younger hunters must have a bird license if they are at least fourteen. Those younger than fourteen actually do not need any stamps or licenses. But they must have a hunter safety card, and their bag limit for waterfowl is included in the total limit for their adult guardian.

If young hunters have their own license and stamp, they will also have their own bag limit. At the beginning of each hunting season, hunters should be sure to check for changes or updates to the state and federal hunting laws and regulations in effect in their area.

Federal Requirements

While individual state fish and wildlife services generally have oversight over the fish, game, and other wildlife within their borders, waterfowl jurisdiction works a bit differently. That's because waterfowl are migratory. That is, they migrate, or travel, to different areas during different seasons and easily cross borders. Since any given waterfowl population makes its home in two or more states throughout the year, the federal government has a responsibility for the waterfowl's well-being and the protection of their habitats. For this reason, the federal government demands certain things of waterfowl hunters over and above any particular state requirements.

Harvest Information Program (HIP)

The Harvest Information Program (HIP) is a federal project in which hunters must participate. There is no fee for participating in the program, but waterfowl hunters complete a mandatory questionnaire in which they are asked to provide accurate information about the number and kind of birds they bagged the previous season.

The questionnaire can be filled out online or in person at any hunting license vendor. The HIP provides federal and state wildlife officials

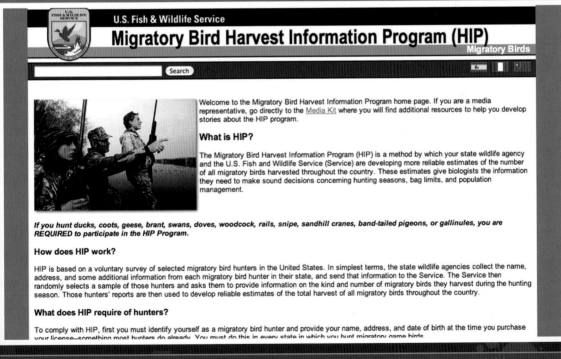

Information on the Migratory Bird Harvest Information Program (HIP) is available online at www.fws.gov/hip. At this site, young hunters can explore some frequently asked questions (FAQs) about why HIP is important.

with valuable information. It aids them in estimating total bird harvests and setting dates for hunting seasons. The data collected by HIP also allows wildlife officials to better protect the health and abundance of waterfowl populations (and therefore the hunters' pastime). They do this by ensuring that overhunting does not occur and the number of waterfowl species does not fall too low. Hunters are required to get HIP certification for each state in which they hunt.

Duck Stamps: Federal and State

All waterfowl hunters are required to get a Federal Migratory Bird Hunting and Conservation Stamp, known as a Duck Stamp. This can be

U.S. Fish & Wildlife Service

The Federal Duck Stamp Program

Since 1934, sales of Federal Duck Stamps to hunters, stamp collectors and other conservationists have raised more than $700 million that has been used to acquire more than 5.2 million acres of habitat for the National Wildlife Refuge System.

About Duck Stamps

View Stamp Images

Federal Duck Stamp Contest

Junior Duck Stamp Program

Your Duck Stamp Dollars at Work

Contact Information

Buy Stamps

Product Information

Home

Information for . . .

○ Search DSO Site

USFWS/Smithsonian Institute

- **What are Duck Stamps?**
- **How do Duck Stamps benefit wildlife?**
- **Why should I buy Duck Stamps?**
- **Where can I buy Duck Stamps and Duck Stamp products?**
- **How are Duck Stamps made?**
- **How can I participate in the Duck Stamp Contest?**
- **Where can I view Duck Stamps?**
- **Who can answer my questions about Duck Stamps?**

What are Duck Stamps?
Federal Migratory Bird Hunting and Conservation Stamps, commonly known as "Duck Stamps," are pictorial stamps produced by the U.S. Postal Service for the U.S. Fish & Wildlife Service. They are not valid for postage. Originally created in 1934 as the federal licenses required for hunting migratory waterfowl, Federal Duck Stamps have a much larger purpose today.

The Federal Duck Stamp Program (www.fws.gov/duckstamps), now administered by the U.S. Fish & Wildlife Service, was started in 1934. This is when Congress decided to raise money through stamp sales for the purpose of acquiring, preserving, and protecting wetlands.

purchased at any U.S. Post Office. All states also require a state duck stamp as well, available at any licensing agent. For convenience, some state licensing agents buy federal duck stamps to resell to hunters so that they can buy both required stamps at one time in one place. But it is not guaranteed that any given state licensing agent will have federal duck stamps on hand.

Hunters must also have a valid state hunting license. This is generally required for each state they plan to hunt in, if more than one. Some states will honor licenses from certain other states, but hunters can't assume this. They need to do the research and find out exactly what licenses and permits they will need to hunt legally in their chosen destination.

Keeping Your Gear Legal

As discussed earlier, rifles and handguns are prohibited in waterfowl hunting. Only shotguns may be used, and many areas restrict the size of the shotgun to no larger than a 10 gauge. The possession and use of steel size T and other shot larger than a BB are often prohibited. It is important that hunters check both state and federal regulations on what kind of shot is legal in their home state or the state of their destination.

In some cases, certain shot may not be used to hunt particular kinds of waterfowl. Yet these restrictions are sometimes lifted temporarily or permanently. The latest updated information on legal and permissible shot can usually be found online, by telephone, or in person at a state fish and wildlife office.

Bag Limits

The amount of any type of waterfowl that can be killed is restricted. Rules vary among states, and even among specific wetland areas within a state, on how many of a certain waterfowl species can be bagged

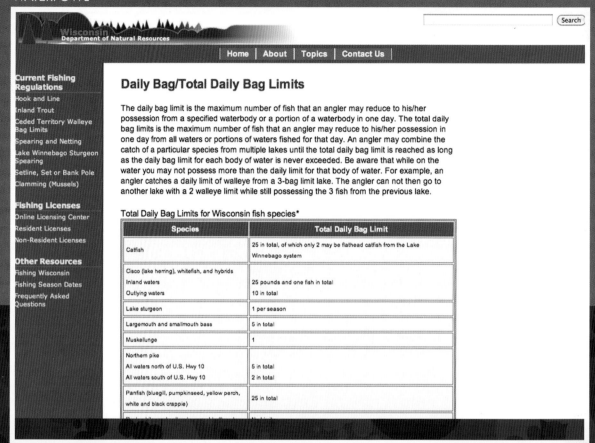

The Wisconsin Department of Natural Resources' Web site (www.dnr.wi.gov) details the bag limits and total limits for both fishers and hunters, including waterfowlers.

during a specific period. This is known as a bag limit. There are daily and seasonal bag limits. There are also differing limits for how many females and males of a species may be shot.

These bag limits change from season to season and are usually set not long before the hunting season opens. Scientists, fish and wildlife officials, and hunters' groups all collect information regarding waterfowl populations and habitats in the months before the hunting season opens. They do this to help determine the proper daily and

While a "No Hunting" sign is the most obvious indicator that hunting is prohibited, waterfowlers must thoroughly investigate which areas are off-limits for hunting. They must also gain clear permission to hunt in any area not explicitly posted as a hunting ground.

seasonal bag limits for each species and sex. Bag limits for each season are posted online and distributed in hard copy to service centers that cater to waterfowlers.

Where Can You Hunt?

Waterfowl hunting takes place in wetland areas where ducks, geese, and other birds stop during their seasonal migrations. There are millions of acres of federal land administered by the U.S. Fish and Wildlife Service (FWS) as National Wildlife Refuges. These refuges are generally open to the public for hunting. In addition, federally controlled Waterfowl Production Areas (WPAs) are known as specific waterfowling destinations. Locally, many state parks and forests are also open to hunting, including special Wildlife Management Areas (WMAs). Individual counties in many states also own and operate public hunting lands.

'Tis the Season ...or Is It?

Waterfowl hunting seasons occur when ducks, geese, and other game birds migrate away from cooling seasonal temperatures and toward feeding grounds in warmer climates. This typically occurs toward the end of summer and early autumn. Consequently, waterfowl hunting seasons may begin anytime from September on.

A typical season may last anywhere from two weeks to two to three months, depending on the breeds of waterfowl involved and the size of their populations in particular states and regions. Permitted hunting of certain birds might even be broken up into a week or weekend at the beginning of autumn and another week later in the season. And different regions within a state may have different hunting seasons. For example, in the western part of New York State, the 2009–2010 season for ducks, coots, and mergansers was October 24 to December 6 and December 16 until January 10. However, these same breeds could only be hunted from October 3 to 11 and October 23 to December 12 in the northeastern part of the state.

However, much of the open land in many states is private property. In some cases, private logging and forest product companies own large parcels of territory but allow hunting. If they do not allow it, the land will be posted or marked with "No Hunting" or "No Trespassing" signs. Hunters must get permission—often in writing—from the landowners in order to hunt on private land. If the hunters are hunting on the land and are asked to leave, they must do so immediately. These trespass laws are vital to the protection of human lives, livestock and wildlife, and property owners' rights. Signs that say "Keep Out," "No Trespassing," or "Hunting Prohibited" are obvious indications that hunting or any other activity is not permitted on that land. Some signs may be posted that say "Ask Permission/See Landowner." In this case, hunting privileges may be granted if the proper permission is sought.

Time Limits

Just as hunting seasons are restricted, so are the times of day when waterfowl hunting is permitted. Most state and hunting areas have strict times when hunting may start in the morning and finish in the evenings. In some states, hunting starts at sunrise and ends at sunset. In others, people may hunt from a half hour before sunrise until an hour after sunset. Once again, specific hours for a state or region are available from game officials and on fish and wildlife Web sites.

CHAPTER 3

GETTING READY AND GEARING UP

One of the most pleasurable aspects of the waterfowling experience is the sense of escape from civilization. Hunters might be trekking through a southern marsh or quietly preparing to shoot a mallard that has flown down to the edge of a prairie pothole, one of those shallow pools in parts of the midwestern Great Plains. Wherever they are hunting, waterfowlers feel far away from the sights, sounds, and stresses of modern life.

Even though it's thrilling and peaceful to escape into the wilderness, hunters must understand the environment they are entering and recognize both its dangers and its fragility. Though it looks beautiful and feels serene, accidents can happen in the wilderness that are potentially life-threatening. And though the wilderness may appear pristine, the human presence within it can be destructive, so care must be taken to minimize one's impact.

It is important to know the environment and the waterfowl that are found there. Waterfowling is done in colder, sometimes subfreezing, weather. Standing in icy water or hunting from a boat for long hours, waiting for an opportunity, requires patience. Ducks and other waterfowl are smart, have great vision, and can see colors. For these reasons, hunters have to rely on their wits, skill, and technique to bag them.

Physical Conditioning

Much of a hunter's time and energy is spent waiting, trying to keep still and hidden. But hunters still need to be in relatively good shape for several reasons. Moving around in the wetland areas favored by waterfowl can be difficult and tiring, and a fair bit of physical effort is required to carry shotguns during an all-day hunt. Decoys, blinds, and other gear can also weigh hunters down. On occasion, they might have to wade through deep water to get where they want to be or retrieve birds they have killed (though waterfowl-hunting dogs are often used for this purpose).

Performing some kind of physical activity daily and eating healthfully will go a long way toward preparing a hunter for the rigors of the great outdoors. It's especially important to eat a good breakfast before going afield and to bring and drink plenty of fluids. Packing trail mix or other high-energy, lightweight foods and snacks is also a good idea. These are useful not only for curbing hunger and thirst during a hunt: if a hunter gets lost or separated from the group, these fluids and snacks may save his or her life.

In Case of Emergency

In addition to guns and gear, a hunting party should always bring along a first-aid kit while in the wilderness. Most waterfowling is done in

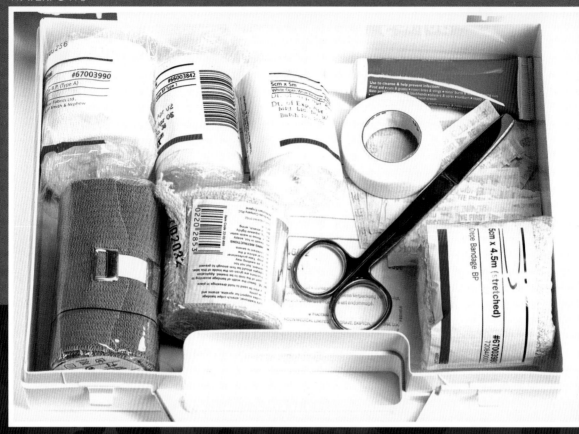

A first-aid/emergency kit is a must for any hunters going afield, even if they are only out briefly. Different types of bandages and ointments can help one treat minor wounds.

relatively safe and accessible areas. Yet hunters in some areas will be out of communication with the outside world and possibly quite far from rescue or the nearest hospital. Plus, if an accident occurs, the person might not be able to move or be moved to get medical help. Even minor injuries benefit greatly from immediate, on-the-spot care.

Ready-made first-aid kits can be purchased at sporting and hunting retailers and at drugstores. They can also be assembled at home. A good one will be waterproof and have disinfectant, first-aid creams and ointments, different kinds of bandages, tweezers, and a first-aid instruction booklet. Scissors or a hunting knife, disposable gloves, an extra flash-light, foil blankets, and numerous other items can also be added.

Shotgun Obstructions

In all the excitement of a hunt, it's often the small, unnoticed hazards that can be the most dangerous. In waterfowl habitats like swamps and grain fields, there is always the chance of bits of debris (leaves, twigs, gravel) getting into the shotgun barrel through the muzzle. Discharging a gun with even a small obstruction in it can be dangerous, even fatal. The barrel could rupture and harm the hunter and those nearby.

If there is an obstruction of some kind in the barrel, it is a good idea for an experienced adult to remove the barrel and check it for block-age. One way is to carry a pull cord, cleaning cord, ramrod, or other tool to keep the barrel clear. Compact gun cleaning kits are also avail-able in sporting good and hunting stores.

Staying Warm and Dry in a Cold, Wet Place

Waterfowl are often hunted when it's chilly, cold, or downright freez-ing, and the birds' habitats are always wet. A waterfowler's mission is to bag some birds while keeping relatively warm and dry.

Before going afield, a hunter should be ready to invest in some weather-resistant and waterproof gear. It almost always pays to spend a little more on high-quality gear, rather than cheaper goods that don't offer as much protection or durability. In some cases, quality gear can make the difference between a successful, safe, and enjoyable hunt and a physically uncomfortable or even dangerous excursion. Hunters who are not equipped with good gear may be forced to abandon the hunt if the weather changes suddenly or unexpectedly.

Pictured here is a well-prepared waterfowler equipped with waterproof boots, camouflage gear, a birdcall, and earmuffs to protect him from the potentially deafening noise of his shotgun.

A hunter's clothing and antiweather gear should include a good pair of sturdy, waterproof boots. Good jackets, gloves, hats, caps, and pants go a long way, too. In addition to being waterproof, good outerwear should offer wind protection. Dressing in layers and bringing extra items of dry clothing are also a good hedge against the cold and damp and sudden shifts in weather.

Most experienced hunters recommend wearing wool or synthetic materials under foul-weather gear, rather than cotton. Cotton absorbs much more water when wet, and this moisture cools the body much faster in cold weather. Cotton is also more abrasive, irritating, and heavy when wet. Unlike cotton, wool can still keep a person warm even when it has become wet.

Mixing and Matching

As veteran Michael Hingle states in an article for *Wildfowl* magazine, "Over time, I've learned to match my camo pattern to each individual situation. For example, I'll never wear a dark pattern in a lighter-colored environment or vice versa. Similarly I would never think of using a snow pattern unless there was snow on the ground. In some situations, I'll wear the same camo pattern from head to toe, yet on other occasions I find it beneficial to mix and match various patterns."

Hingle adds that he avoids camouflage with shiny buttons because they reflect light in a way that ducks find unnatural. A bigger mistake would be to hunt with fluorescent-orange vests, which are used in some other types of game hunting. In waterfowl hunting, fluorescent orange serves as a huge warning sign for ducks that humans are present.

Hypothermia, a potentially deadly condition in which one's core body temperature drops too low for normal metabolic and bodily functions, can set in at even above-freezing temperatures. These days, well-designed synthetic clothing that is lightweight, comfortable, and quick-drying is available for going afield. Bringing along a complete change of clothes just in case a hunter falls into water or otherwise gets drenched is also recommended.

Protecting Your Ears

A waterfowler's ears are among his or her most important tools while hunting. Since hearing is also vitally important in everyday life, it is essential for hunters to protect their ears. Earplugs are a must to help avoid the permanent hearing loss that can occur as a result of firing guns.

Priority One: Waders

Waders are one of the must-have items for waterfowling. These are one-piece waterproof pants and boots worn over regular pants and shoes while standing in water or moving through wet and muddy terrain. There are two types: hip waders and chest-high waders. Chest-high waders are recommended for the greater coverage they offer, keeping hunters dry even when they are crouching or sitting in water, very damp ground, or wet vegetation.

Waders are made from different kinds of synthetic material, such as neoprene, nylon, or Gore-Tex. In addition to keeping the wearer dry, good waders will have spacious, watertight pockets that can hold shotgun shells, bird calls, and other items. As with other gear, it is best to spend a little more money on a good pair of waders that will keep a hunter dryer, warmer, and better insulated than a cheap pair will.

U.S. Olympic trap shooter Bret Erickson holds two spent shell casings after competing. Proper care of firearms and disposal of spent shot casings are an important part of any waterfowl outing.

Camouflage: Hiding in Plain Sight

Another must when hunting is camouflage. Ducks, in particular, see colors and have very good vision. They are also very perceptive and can often sense when something looks unusual or suspicious. Any hint of the presence of human beings makes them anxious and wary—or scares them off entirely. That's why a hunter's outerwear should easily blend into the surrounding environment. Hunters have a wide range of camouflage patterns to choose from. Modern camo closely replicates the natural, irregular patterns of shading, light, and color found in field and stream.

CHAPTER 4

GOING AFIELD

The only way to learn all the ins and outs of waterfowl hunting is by actually doing it, and that means going afield. From weather and water safety to decoys, calls, and blinds, there is a lot to learn, much field experience to gain, and a lot of fun and adventure to be had.

Fowl Weather

Learning about how weather affects waterfowl provides larger clues to their behavior, allowing for a more successful hunt. How do ducks react to weather, and how can hunters use this knowledge?

A storm front is good news for waterfowl hunters. Storms can mean harsher winds, rain, sleet, snow, and cloud cover. In these kinds of stormy conditions, ducks keep moving to find shelter. They then gather in

Taking advantage of the favorable duck hunting weather, hunters with a Labrador retriever bird dog watch overcast skies for migrating birds in a floodplain in Stuttgart, Arkansas.

these sheltered areas—like hillsides and lake coves—where they are easier to track. They also fly lower, where the winds are less powerful, which means they're at closer range.

Cloud cover also helps duck hunters stay hidden. The sun does not reflect off the barrels of guns or other surfaces that reveal the presence of hunters. Even the light reflected off human faces can alert a bird to danger, and the shadows cast by hunters are also telltale signs of their presence.

When it's sunny, hunting conditions worsen. Ducks fly higher and are less restricted in their movements. They spot faces reflecting the sunlight and more easily notice the slightest movements and silhouettes. Just as hunters learn more and more about waterfowl behavior over time, ducks, too, learn about the behavior of the hunters. A few days of nice weather can help them better learn how to avoid getting bagged.

A well-concealed hunter aims his shotgun from within a blind constructed of, and camouflaged by, natural materials such as reeds and marsh hay.

Blinds

Even well-disguised humans can stick out like a sore thumb. That's why hunters construct blinds out in the field to better hide themselves. A blind is any human-made structure that conceals hunters from their prey.

A natural blind can be constructed from elements gathered in the immediate environment, like sticks, leaves, and reeds. Some hunters even grow or harvest their own wood before hitting the field to "brush" their blinds. This saves them the trouble of finding brush where they hunt, which might not necessarily be available. Others even dig pits and camouflage them with things like cornstalks. They then crouch down in the pit to wait for duck or geese.

Some blinds are constructed of wood that is camouflaged, either with natural materials or with camo similar to that which hunters wear. People even build more complex, even luxurious, blinds, which have heating and other modern conveniences that protect hunters from foul weather.

Decoys

Humans need to trick waterfowl into feeling safe enough to land nearby or gather within range. One important way to do this is with the help of decoys.

Decoys are realistic replicas of ducks and other waterfowl that hunters place in the water and other places where they want to attract live birds. For real birds, decoys create the illusion that other birds have gathered safely, away from humans and other predators. This makes them drop their guard and land nearby, within range of the hunters.

Goose decoys decorate a frozen lake in midwinter. Hunters lurk close by, hoping that their fake geese look convincing enough for real geese to let their guard down and land nearby.

Weighted-Keel vs. Water-Keel Decoys

Decoys can be made from wood, cork, and other buoyant materials, but the most common and realistic ones are made from plastic. Plastic decoys have the added advantage of being widely available and affordable. In water, plastic line is used to connect decoys to each other and to the hunter. If a line is not used, the decoys will float away from each other and beyond the hunter's desired location. This would also make it very hard to collect and retrieve the decoys.

A Natural Spread

Every hunter has a different decoying technique, or several techniques, depending on the birds involved, the weather, the location, and other circumstances. There's no rule of thumb, exactly. Different kinds of waterfowl respond differently, and this can change according to the environment, weather, and general "mood." Hunters watch how ducks respond to decoys and change the arrangements of them in response. A decoy arrangement is known as a spread or set.

For example, Michael Hingle tells *Wildfowl* magazine that he gained insight into decoying through experience. Earlier, he had always set decoys too close together. He says, "It finally dawned on me that ducks and geese spread out when relaxed and moved closer together when they become alarmed or nervous." By spreading his decoys out more loosely, in groups of four to seven, with 3 feet (0.9 m) separating each decoy, Hingle attracted more birds. In addition, he also arranged a "landing zone" for incoming birds, making them more comfortable with landing, or "committing," in waterfowling language.

There are two main types of decoys: weighted-keel and water-keel. Water-keel decoys are hollow or made so that water will flow through them (though some are designed to fill up). Weighted-keel decoys are filled with sand and sealed and thus are heavier, which is a disadvantage if a hunter is lugging around dozens of them. But when tossed or placed in the water, they set, or right themselves, better. Their weight also makes them appear to swim more naturally, an important illusion when fooling real ducks. For these reasons, weighted-keel decoys are far more commonly used.

Water-keel decoys do have some advantages, however. They are lighter and more easily transported, meaning more decoys can be brought along. Newer models actually are better at setting themselves and remaining upright, and their "swimming" motions have become more lifelike. Also, because of their lower weight, water-keel decoys move more freely and naturally on days with light wind. Some hunters employ homemade methods to convert a water-keel decoy to a weighted-keel. Weighted straps, available for sale or fashioned at home, can be added as desired. These straps can be useful to keep decoys upright in various and changing wind conditions.

The decoys used by hunters should be matched to the birds being hunted. If resources are limited, however, and only a few decoys can be purchased and/or brought along, mallard decoys are the best bet, since many waterfowl species respond well to them. With decoys, more is usually better, and a greater variety of decoys often works best in creating spreads that will make real birds commit.

Calling All Waterfowl

Another important tool in a hunter's arsenal is the duck or goose call. Calls are woodwind instruments, consisting of a barrel, a sounding

New Zealand waterfowler Brian Thomson works his duck call during a hunt in Mercer, near Auckland. Many hunters consider good calling an art.

board, and a reed. One uses a duck call to attract ducks to land or have them fly within shooting range. Waterfowl calls range in price from very cheap to quite expensive, but good ones can be found that are fairly inexpensive.

Different waterfowl species respond differently to calls at different times and under different conditions. For mallards, one of the most commonly hunted ducks, the call replicates the natural call of the hen (female). It should be sounded louder at a distance and quieter as the mallards close in. Mallard hens make the common "quacking" sound most people associate with ducks. Other waterfowl, such as pintail, teal, wood ducks, and the mallard drake (male), make a whistling sound.

Overcalling can make birds wary, but a well-placed response to a hen leading a flock can encourage the birds to commit. Keith McCutcheon advises readers of *Ducks Unlimited* magazine to "use your call sparingly. If more people approached it that way, it would be better on them, and on other hunters as well."

Dogs: A Waterfowler's Best Friend

Hunters can go afield without one, but there's nothing like a good waterfowl dog to retrieve downed birds. A well-trained canine is a hunter's best friend, while an impatient, undisciplined, or disobedient one can scare ducks and geese away. However, one must always have patience, especially with a dog in training. Most of the dog's training should be done at home, not afield.

There are many benefits to bringing along a dog. Besides being natural swimmers, most bird dogs are very obedient and eager to please. A good one will keep quiet during the crucial moments of the hunt that require stealth. Dogs can withstand cold water and weather better than humans and are essential when retrieving birds in particularly dangerous conditions. With their keen sense of smell, dogs are expert at finding and retrieving birds.

There are several breeds of dogs that are common in waterfowling, chosen for their temperament, intelligence, and ease of training. Golden retrievers are among the most popular, as are cocker spaniels, springer spaniels, and Labrador retrievers. With a little bit of discipline, and a lot of care, a dog can become an eager bird retriever and loving and loyal pet for years to come.

Raising and training a good bird dog is a must for any serious waterfowler, as it makes a hunt so much safer and easier. Here, a brown Labrador retriever sits patiently with a bird it has retrieved.

Boats and Hunting on Water

Much waterfowl hunting is done from a boat. Only certain kinds of watercraft can be used for hunting, however. Rules vary among states, but waterfowlers can usually only shoot from rowboats and similar craft that are human-propelled. That is, motor-driven craft or sailboats are sometimes restricted. In cases where they are allowed, the motor must be shut off or the sail furled while shooting.

For waterfowling purposes, a boat requires concealment. Boat blinds are used, many times by using the natural terrain as cover. For example, using dense vegetation, whether on water or along shore-lines to mask the boat's presence, goes a long way to fooling the birds overhead or swimming nearby.

A boat blind may be brought along, or it may even be part of the construction of the boat itself. Boats allow hunters greater freedom of movement, getting them out on the water and into the sheltered places where waterfowl feed or otherwise gather. But boat hunting can also be dangerous. When out on the water, remember that one's safety and that of the entire hunting party are the most important thing.

Boat Safety

The dangers of boat hunting include falling into the water and capsizing the boat itself. In cold conditions, this is especially dangerous. Even with waterproof apparel, a hunter can develop hypothermia or drown when weighed down by equipment and gear and several layers of wet and increasingly heavy clothing. A hunter's excitement in getting that perfect spot on the water, or getting a good shot in, can cloud judgment while on a boat, with tragic consequences.

The boat should be equipped with safety and emergency items, including:

• Life vests and a flotation/rescue device that can be thrown to someone who has fallen into the water
• Visual and sound-producing signal devices in case of emergency, like flares, whistles, and air horns
• A fire extinguisher
• A first-aid kit
• Spare sets of dry and warm clothing

It is also absolutely necessary that the boat have a waterproof container or compartment where these emergency and lifesaving items can be safely stored, along with other gear.

CHAPTER 5

Bagging, Tagging, and Clearing Out

The preparations have been made, the gear has been packed, and the equipment has been moved into place in the field. Now all that remains is the most important part of all: bagging the ducks or geese.

Ready, Aim, Fire: Three Kinds of Shooting

There are three basic techniques for hunting waterfowl: jump shooting, pass shooting, and hunting over decoys. Jump shooting means sneaking into shotgun range of birds that are feeding or resting, often in small ponds, streams, or irrigation canals. When the birds discover a hunter's presence, they will start flying away, which is when a hunter should take his or her shot.

Pass shooting involves hunters taking positions in areas where they anticipate that

Properly preparing a well-camouflaged blind and shelter, as this hunter is doing, is an important part of a successful waterfowl outing. Note how well the hunter's clothing, shelter, and surrounding environment blend together.

waterfowl will fly by. This technique gets the best results on windier days, when birds fly low.

Hunting over decoys is perhaps the most widely practiced and classic way to bag waterfowl. Decoys are spread, the caller attracts the birds, and the camouflaged hunters wait in a blind.

Shooting Tips and Tricks

All hunters have their own shooting styles and techniques. Beyond the essential rules of gun safety, there are several important guidelines to follow to help ensure a more successful hunt and avoid common waterfowl shooting mistakes.

Taking Your Time

A common mistake is shooting too quickly in fear that birds will flare out of range. This often leads to errant shots and missing the targeted ducks and geese. Waiting just that extra two seconds after the birds have noticed the hunter leaves him or her with enough time to take a few shots before the waterfowl fly out of range. The shotgun should be mounted fluidly. Remember, this is not a quick-draw, fastest-trigger-finger contest.

One at a Time

Another bit of advice is to aim for one bird at a time, rather than flock shooting. Pick one bird and concentrate on it, rather than switching targets. As Wade Bourne notes wisely in an article for *Ducks Unlimited* magazine, "An incoming flight of ducks is 95 percent air." This means a hunter is more likely to drop a bird by taking his or her time and aiming at only one member of the flock.

A hunter takes aim at a passing duck as decoys float in the water near his feet. The proper use, deployment, and spread of decoys can dramatically increase a waterfowler's chance of bagging a bird.

Beginning hunters might like to focus their attention on the closest, lowest, and easiest target. Aiming for a trailing bird, says Bourne, will put the hunter in position to try again with second and third shots as other birds in the flock flare up.

Leading a Bird

Bourne advises hunters to concentrate on the front of the target. On long, passing shots, most hunters will lead with their rifle ahead of the bird. Those who don't will often take shots that pass behind the bird.

Decoying Waterfowl

Using decoys creatively and intelligently can make a huge difference in getting off good shots. Typically, decoys should be placed no farther away than 40 to 45 yards (37 to 41 m). They should be set up in a shape that gives the birds a landing zone. Birds land into, not away from, the wind, so the hunter should have the wind at his or her back. This way, the birds will approach the decoys from in front of the hunter.

Shooting at birds that are too far off—some call it "skybusting"—is a common mistake. Twenty to 30 yards (18 to 27 m) is an ideal range for most. At that distance, a hunter can clearly make out a duck's eyeballs. If the bird's eyeballs cannot be seen, chances are it is still too far away and too early to take a shot.

Gun Safety Reminders

Always remember the Ten Commandments of Firearms Safety covered in chapter 1. Among other rules, hunters should always ensure that their shotgun safety catch is on at all times and only released when it is time to shoot. When loading the gun, keep the muzzle pointed up. In the blind, guns should be stored vertically and should not rest across a hunter's lap.

Hunters should always be mindful of their hunting partners when preparing to shoot. The hunting party should agree ahead of time on each hunter's planned line of fire. If one hunter is shooting near someone else in a blind or elsewhere, he or she must be conscious of muzzle blast. Never shoot near or over a hunting partner. Stay in the blind during any shooting. When going out to retrieve a downed bird, a hunter should make sure to alert everyone and confirm that they have heard him or her and will hold their fire.

Good and Bad Sportsmanship

One of the reasons why skybusting is a bad practice relates to simple good sportsmanship. If the aim of waterfowl hunting was simply to bag as many birds as possible, firing a machine gun from a tank would be acceptable. But shooting faraway targets with a shotgun increases the risk of merely crippling or otherwise injuring the birds, leading to a slow and painful death. There is no need to make a living creature suffer needlessly.

By the same token, other rules exist that ensure waterfowlers behave in a sportsmanlike manner. That's why, in many or all states, waterfowlers cannot:

- Hunt from a floating blind that is not anchored
- Use high-powered weaponry or explosives
- Use poison, drugs, or traps
- Chase birds on motor-conveyed vehicles
- Use electronic calling devices
- Use live, trapped birds as living decoys

Most hunters naturally consider such techniques to be unsportsmanlike or cruel.

Dressing a Bird

After a hunter bags a duck or goose and his or her faithful dog has retrieved the bird from the reeds, what happens next? It depends on what the hunters want to do with the bird. If they plan to eat the duck or goose, they need to dress the bird. This means readying it for transport and consumption by removing certain feathers and internal body parts.

It's important to keep the birds' bodies cool, so if the hunters have bagged several ducks or geese, they need to keep them separate and not stacked in a pile, for example. The birds should be laid out individually or hung up (in a blind, for instance) with duck straps.

Waterfowl are relatively easy to dress. It is generally done at home, but may also be done in the field. First, the feathers on the bird's lower breast and abdomen need to be plucked. Using a knife, cut through the skin of its belly at the base of the breast area. Bend the bird backward and remove its entrails, or nonedible organs. Finally, pluck the remaining feathers and remove its feathery cape. The bird must be dried and kept cool, generally by putting it on ice in a cooler for transport.

To identify the bagged birds, all states require that the hunter either leaves the head or one wing, or both, on each bird brought in. This way, gaming officials can ensure that hunters are complying with bag limits on certain species and sexes.

For complete safety from contact with any possible germs or diseases, hunters need to wear latex gloves or some other protection while dressing birds in the field. While dressing a bird, a hunter should avoid eating, drinking, or other activities that might make him or her inadvertently touch his or her face. Keep the carcass and its fluids away from other food and drinks.

Finally, make sure to thoroughly clean and disinfect the tools used for dressing birds. While the contagious HPAI H5N1 flu virus—known as avian or bird flu—has not yet been detected in North American waterfowl, it is better to be safe than sorry.

When dressing a bird and preparing it for storage or a meal, several techniques can be used to remove its feathers. The bird can be plucked by hand or with the help of a mechanical plucking device. Soaking a carcass in near-scalding water a few times (without accidentally starting to cook it) makes feather removal much easier. Another method is to wax the bird. The bird can also be skinned or filleted.

Tagging a Bird

One of the ways that authorities enforce bag limits is with the requirement that each person tags his or her birds before either transporting them home or to a migratory bird preservation facility.

In North Carolina, for example, it is required that a bird—with either its head or one wing intact—be tagged with the hunter's signature, address, total number of birds tagged according to species and sex, and the dates of the kills. This includes any birds taken by the hunter or transferred to another person. Live or injured fowl that have been retrieved must be killed and included in a hunter's daily bag limit. If shipping birds, the outside of the shipment must have the names and addresses of both the sender and the recipient.

Happy Hunting!

Having become prepared to get out there and take part in the popular sport and tradition of waterfowl hunting, remember to keep safe, abide by all the relevant rules and codes of ethics, and, above all, have fun. Relatives, older siblings, family friends, and mentors will be happy to answer any questions or concerns that may arise. They can help provide safe, educational, and rewarding hunting experiences. So start getting ready for the coming season, and happy hunting!

GLOSSARY

afield Short for "going afield," refers to being in a waterfowl hunting area.

bag limit The daily and seasonal maximum limit allowed for killing specific numbers of particular waterfowl species.

blind The concealing shelter, made from various types of materials, in which hunters lie in wait for waterfowl.

bore The shaft or barrel of the shotgun through which shot travels and then exits through the muzzle.

call A woodwind tool that lets hunters mimic the sounds that waterfowl make in order to attract them better.

commitment The decision of lured waterfowl to land within firing range in response to calling and decoying.

decoy A realistic replica of a duck or other waterfowl used to attract birds within shooting range; also can be used as a verb, as in "to decoy" a pond.

drake A male duck.

duck stamp One of the federal and state certifications that hunters must obtain to hunt during a particular season.

flyways The migratory routes, usually with easy access to wet areas, that waterfowl travel seasonally.

gauge The size of a shotgun's bore, which affects its shooting power.

Harvest Information Program (HIP) The obligatory and free federal certification program that aids the federal government in determining annual waterfowl populations and harvest limits.

hen A female duck.

skybusting Shooting birds that are too far away to effectively hit or kill.

smoothbore A weapon in which the interior of the bore is smooth, contrasted with rifles, which are grooved, or rifled, within.

spread An arrangement of decoys; sometimes referred to as a set.

tagging The process of marking possession of birds by the hunter who bagged them; this is done to ensure proper compliance with bag limits.

waders Waterproof pants, often with attached boots, worn over the clothes, which protect the waterfowler from cold water and the elements in general.

waterfowl Migratory birds whose natural habitats are the wetlands and other wet areas of the world.

Waterfowl Production Area (WPA) Federally protected waterfowl hunting area that is part of the U.S. Fish and Wildlife Service's National Wildlife Refuge System. All WPAs provide habitat for a vast variety of waterfowl, shorebirds, grassland birds, plants, insects, and wildlife. They also help reduce erosion, clean and protect ground water, and reduce flooding. WPAs provide opportunities for public access and recreation such as hunting, wildlife watching, and photography.

water-keel Decoys that are lighter than weighted-keel decoys and hollowed out so that water may flow through them.

weighted-keel Decoys that are sealed and are heavier and easier to keep upright in water than are water-keel decoys.

Canadian Wildlife Service (CWS)

Environment Canada

Ottawa, ON K1A 0H3

Canada

(800) 668-6767

Web site: http://www.cws-scf.ec.gc.ca/index_e.cfm

The CWS is the wildlife and hunting division of Environment Canada.

Delta Waterfowl

Unit 22-62 Scurfield Boulevard

Winnipeg, MB R3Y 1M5

Canada

(877) 667-5656

Web site: http://www.deltawaterfowl.org

Delta Waterfowl is a major North American organization, based in Canada, whose mission is to secure the future of waterfowl and waterfowl hunting.

Ducks Unlimited

One Waterfowl Way

Memphis, TN 38120

(800) 45-DUCKS [453-8257]

Web site: http://www.ducks.org

Ducks Unlimited is a leading international organization that helps preserve wetlands, waterfowl, and the hunting tradition.

Ducks Unlimited Canada

P.O. Box 1160

Stonewall, MB R0C 2Z0

Canada

(800) 665-DUCK [3825]

Web site: http://www.ducks.ca

This is the Canadian branch of Ducks Unlimited.

U.S. Fish and Wildlife Service (USFWS)

Department of the Interior

4401 Fairfax Drive

Arlington, VA 22203-1622

(703) 358-1718

Web site: http://www.fws.gov

The USFWS is the federal government's department in charge of conservation and game hunting, including waterfowl.

Waterfowl U.S.A.

National Headquarters

Box 50

The Waterfowl Building

Edgefield, SC 29824

(803) 637-5767

Web site: http://www.waterfowlusa.org

Waterfowl U.S.A. is a nonprofit organization promoting waterfowl conservation. It publishes *Waterfowl* magazine for its members.

Web Sites

Due to the changing nature of Internet links, Rosen Publishing has developed an online list of Web sites related to the subject of this book. This site is updated regularly. Please use this link to access the list:

http://www.rosenlinks.com/hunt/wafo

FOR FURTHER READING

Burch, Monte. *The Ultimate Guide to Calling and Decoying Waterfowl: Tips and Tactics for Hunting Ducks and Geese*. Guilford, CT: The Lyons Press, 2004.

Earley, Chris G. *Waterfowl of Eastern North America*. Richmond Hill, ON, Canada: Firefly Books, 2005.

Frähm, David J. *Duck Hunting* (Edge Books). Mankato, MN: Capstone Press, 2007.

Johnson, Julia. *Waterfowling: Beyond the Basics*. Mechanicsburg, PA: Stackpole Books, 2008.

Klein, Adam G. *Hunting* (Outdoor Adventure). Edina, MN: Checkerboard Books, 2008.

MacRae, Sloan. *Upland Hunting: Pheasant, Quail, and Other Game Birds* (Open Season). New York, NY: PowerKids Press, 2010.

MacRae, Sloan. *Waterfowl Hunting* (Open Season). New York, NY: PowerKids Press, 2010.

Martin, Michael. *Pheasant Hunting* (Edge Books). Mankato, MN: Capstone Press, 2007.

Miller, Warren Hastings. *The American Hunting Dog: Modern Strains of Bird Dogs and Hounds, and Their Field Training*. Berlin, Germany: NABU Press, 2010.

Smith, Nick. *Waterfowl Hunting: Ducks and Geese of North America* (The Complete Hunter). Minneapolis, MN: Creative Publishing international, 2006.

Spencer, Jim. *A Young Hunter's Guide to Waterfowling and Conservation*. Memphis, TN: Ducks Unlimited, 2004.

Bibby, Marvin D. "Duck Hunting School Now in Session." *Game & Fish*. Retrieved February 2010 (http://www.gameandfishmag.com/hunting/ducks-geese-hunting/gf_aa106602a).

Bourne, Wade. "10 Shooting Tips for Waterfowl." Ducks Unlimited. Retrieved February 2010 (http://www.ducks.org/Hunting/BetterWaterfowlingTips/2798/10ShootingTipsforWaterfowl.html).

Bourne, Wade. "Live to Hunt Another Day: Waterfowl Hunters Must Keep Safety in Mind as They Pursue Their Pleasures." Ducks Unlimited. Retrieved February 2010 (http://www.ducks.org/Hunting/HuntingTips/3955/SafetyFirstLivetoHuntAnotherDay.html?poe=huntingtips).

Bourne, Wade. "Waterfowler's Notebook: Outfitting a Duck Boat." Ducks Unlimited, March/April 2010. Retrieved March 2010 (http://www.ducks.org/DU_Magazine/DUMagazineMarApr2010/4847/OutfittingaDuckBoat.html?poe=magLanding).

Delta Waterfowl. "Tips on Duck Calling." Retrieved February 2010 (http://www.deltawaterfowl.org/hunting/calling.php).

Everhart, Johnny. "Lessons in Waterfowling #1: Basic Fowl Language." MissouriOutback.com. Retrieved February 2010 (http://www.missourioutback.com/Stories/lesson1.html).

Everhart, Johnny. "Lessons in Waterfowling #2: Decoy Basics." MissouriOutback.com. Retrieved February 2010 (http://www.missourioutback.com/Stories/lesson2.html).

Hendricks, Bryan. "Finding Waterfowl Hotspots That Others Miss." Game & Fish. Retrieved February 2010 (http://www.gameandfishmag.com/hunting/ducks-geese-hunting/gf_aa116403a).

Johnson, Julia. *Waterfowling: Beyond the Basics*. Mechanicsburg, PA: Stackpole Books, 2008.

McKee, Jennifer. "Wildlife Agency Takes Up Lead Ammo Ban This Week." *Billings Gazette*, February 8, 2010. Retrieved February 2010 (http://billingsgazette.com/news/state-and-regional/montana/article_7f364060-1513-11df-9e8f-001cc4c002e0.html).

Miller, Sarah Swan. *Waterfowl: From Swans to Screamers* (Animals in Order). London, England: Franklin Watts, 2000.

North Carolina Wildlife Resources Commission. "North Carolina General Rules for Hunting." Retrieved February 2010 (http://www.ncwildlife.org/hunting/wf_gen_hunt_info.htm).

Olson, Rob. "Youth Hunting: Our Kids Deserve Nothing Less." Delta Waterfowl, February 2007. Retrieved February 2010 (http://www.deltawaterfowl.org/media/magazine/archive/2007-02/hunting.php).

Pass, Aaron Fraser. "How to Pick the Right Shotgun for Young Duck Hunters." Ducks Unlimited. Retrieved February 2010 (http://www.ducks.org/Hunting/ShootingTips/175/PickingtheRightShotgunforYoungDuckHunters.html?poe=shooting).

Remington Rifle Company. "The Ten Commandments of Firearms Safety." Retrieved February 2010 (http://www.remington.com/pages/news-and-resources/safety-center/10-commandments.aspx).

Remington Rifle Company. "Waterfowl Shooting Tips." Retrieved February 2010 (http://www.remington.com/pages/news-and-resources/safety-center/safety-and-shooting-tips/waterfowl-shooting-tips.aspx).

Smith, Steve. *Hunting Ducks and Geese: Hard Facts, Good Bets, and Serious Advice from a Duck Hunter You Can Trust*. Mechanicsburg, PA: Stackpole Books, 2003.

State of Minnesota Department of Natural Resources. "Hunting Safety Tips." Retrieved February 2010 (http://www.dnr.state.mn.us/hunting/tips/safety.html).

Stuckey, Mike. "In Many States, Young Kids May Hunt Alone." MSNBC, July 21, 2009. Retrieved February 2010 (http://www.msnbc.msn.com/id/31952727/ns/us_news-life).

Sutton, Keith. "Forecast Your Duck Hunting Success." Ducks Unlimited. Retrieved February 2010 (http://www.ducks.org/Hunting/HuntingTips/3431/ForecastYourDuckHuntingSuccess.htm).

Wexo, John Bonnett. *Ducks, Geese, & Swans* (Zoobooks Series). Poway, CA: Wildlife Education, Ltd., 1998.

Wisconsin State Department of Natural Resources. "Waterfowl Regulations—How Are They Set?" Retrieved February 2010 (http://www.dnr.state.wi.us/org/land/wildlife/hunt/waterfow/process.htm).

Young, Matt, ed. *161 Waterfowling Secrets*. Memphis, TN: Ducks Unlimited, 2002.

INDEX

About the Author

Philip Wolny is a writer and editor living in New York. As a child, he spent a considerable amount of time in the company of duck hunters during vacations in Tennessee.

About the Consultant

Benjamin Cowan has over twenty years of both big game and small game hunting experience. In addition to being an avid hunter, Mr. Cowan is also a member of many conservation organizations. He currently resides in west Tennessee.

Photo Credits

Cover, pp. 1, 3, 12, 14, 23, 30, 43, 47 Shutterstock; background art (camouflage) © www.istockphoto.com/Dar Yang Yan; back cover (background), chapter art, sidebar art © www.istockphoto.com/Jason Lugo; back cover (silhouette), chapter art (silhouette) Hemera/Thinkstock; chapter art (silhouette) © istockphoto.com/Michael Olson; pp. 5, 41 Sandra Mu/Getty Images; p. 8 © AP Images; p. 10 Jupiter Images/Comstock/Thinkstock; p. 17 Michigan Department of Natural Resources and Environment; pp. 19, 20 U.S. Fish & Wildlife Service; p. 22 Wisconsin Department of Natural Resources; p. 28 Stephen Smith/Photonica/Getty Images; p. 33 Ezra Shaw/Getty Images; p. 35 William Albert Allard/National Geographic/Getty Images; p. 36 Viktor Drachev/AFP/Getty Images; p. 38 Mike Kemp Images/The Image Bank/Getty Images; p. © Dennis Hallinan/Hulton Archive/Getty Images.

Designer: Nicole Russo, Photo Researcher: Marty Levick